The Family Hand-Me-Down Book

Creating and Preserving Family Traditions

Debbie Trafton O'Neal ✦ Illustrations by Dana Regan

Augsburg Books
Bringing Families Together
for Children & Families

To families everywhere:

May you appreciate, celebrate, and enjoy one another each and every day!

With special love and thanks to my mom, who always kept our family centered and gave so much of herself in all that she did. I love you, Mom!

THE FAMILY HAND-ME-DOWN BOOK
Creating and Preserving Family Traditions

Cover design by Derek Herzog
Book design by Michelle L. Norstad

Library of Congress Cataloging-in-Publication Data
The family hand-me-down book
　　p. cm.
　ISBN 0-8066-4035-9
　1. Handicraft. 2. Cookery. 3. Family—Miscellanea.
TT157.F36 2000
745.5—dc21　　　　　　　　　　　　　99-058204

The paper used in this publication meets the minimum requirements of American National Standard for Information Sciences—Permanence of Paper for Printed Library Materials, ANSI Z329.48-1984. ⊗™

Printed and bound in Hong Kong by C & C Offset Printing Co., Ltd.　　　　　　　　AF 9-4035

04　　03　　02　　01　　00　　1　　2　　3　　4　　5　　6　　7　　8　　9　　10

Contents

INTRODUCTION

Nothing is more precious than the time we spend with our families. Yet the world we live in and the lives we lead often seem to conspire against family togetherness. Our days are filled with one scheduled event after another. How can we carve out time for being together with our families?

This book is all about making time for family—about ways to create and celebrate family traditions. Every family I talk to has special traditions and fun things they do "just because." Some of their traditions go way back: a recipe always shared on Christmas Eve or a card game handed down through generations. Other traditions ebb and flow as families grow and change. Memory-making moments may be impromptu occasions that take only a fraction of our day, or they may be annual events that are much anticipated and savored for months.

The family that creates, observes, and hands down traditions—holiday customs, attitudes of courtesy and good humor, games, prayer and faith rituals, special foods and recipes, favorite stories and quotations—builds unity, strength, and a unique identity into its members. And families that honor and share traditions discover that life is a little more fun and a lot more meaningful.

This book is just a beginning; the ideas here are only starters. I don't think I could even scratch the surface of all of the important things that can be enjoyed, shared, and then handed down to the people we love most. Try out suggestions that appeal to you; let them trigger ideas of your own, or see if they bring back memories of family traditions from your own childhood—traditions you might want to reclaim and celebrate anew.

At the end of each theme section is a "Notes" page for your own thoughts and ideas. Jot down things you want to try, ways you can adapt or personalize suggestions, helpful books and resources to consult, recipes or games from your own family, dates and events and people to remember and celebrate. Then get busy building traditions.

Finally, this book is all about celebrating life. God gives us each new day to laugh, to sing, to listen, to discover new things—to celebrate! God gives us traditions to link us to the past and to the future. And God gives us people to celebrate traditions with.

Won't you join me in celebrating—and in handing down—the best of family traditions?

Debbie Trafton O'Neal

DEBBIE TRAFTON O'NEAL

FAMILY ROOTS

In this day and age when family members are often scattered around the globe, it becomes more and more important to keep a record of our roots—stories of ancestors who helped shape the history and traditions of our families. If you were as blessed as I was with a grandmother who was the family storykeeper, you already know some events, people, and places that make your family unique. But you probably don't know all of them.

You have the challenge to help preserve old stories and create new ones, to pass on traditions and rituals for generations to come. As you begin the discovery process, you will be creating memories and planting family roots of your own.

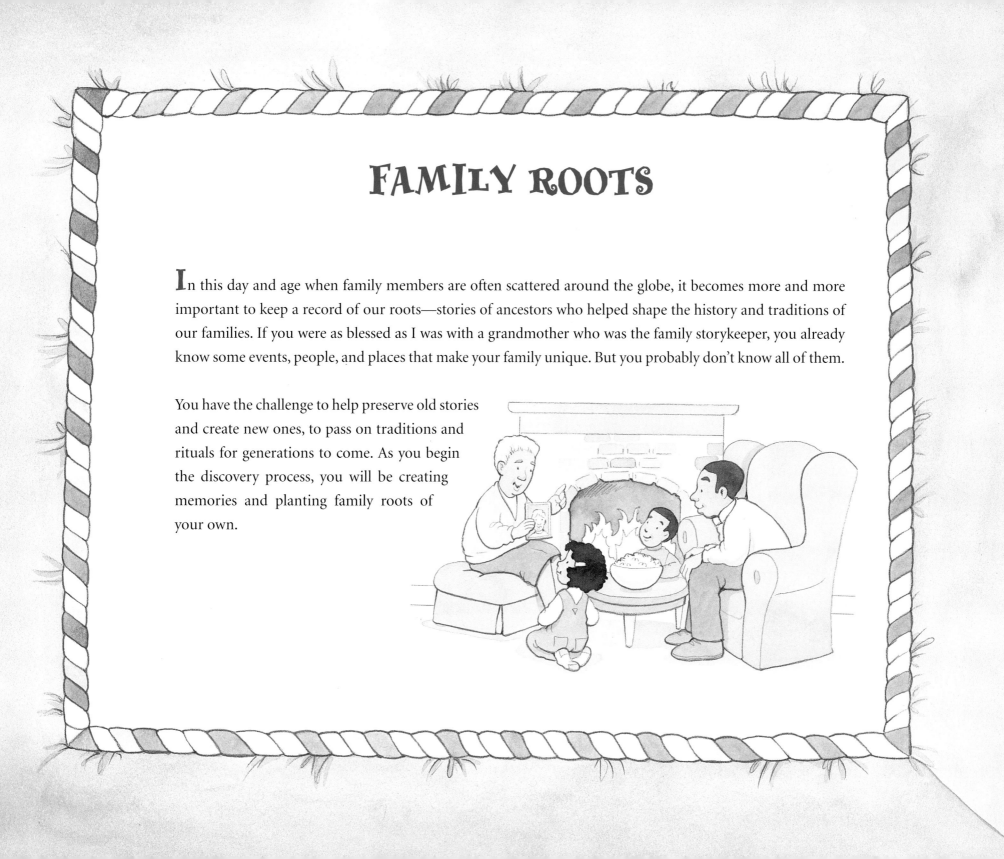

Oral Histories

There are several ways to make oral histories, and each way has as many variations as your family can come up with. Not only does an oral history preserve the stories and voices of family members, it also lets everyone see how family history helped make them who they are. Interviewing a family member is an excellent way to make an oral history.

First determine whom you will interview: Grandpa? Mom? Uncle Bill? Decide if you want to make an audiotape or a videotape, then gather the equipment you'll need. To get things started, you might make a list of questions and give these to the interviewees ahead of time so they can start thinking. Although your "history" may be clearer if one person does the interviewing, it can be fun

to have a group of family interviewers contribute questions and laughter throughout the tape.

When you are finished, label the tapes with names and dates, and perhaps a photo of the interviewer(s) and interviewee. Include a summary of the questions asked, and be sure to make a copy of the tape for the person who was interviewed. Play the recordings at family reunions or holiday gatherings.

Here are questions to get you started:

+ Where did you grow up? What was your house like?
+ What did you enjoy doing when you were my age? What was your favorite school subject? Who was your favorite teacher?
+ What are your earliest/happiest memories? Did you have any pets?
+ How and where did you meet your future husband/wife? What were your first impressions of him/her?
+ Where did you live when you were an adult?
+ What is one thing you have always wanted to do but never have?

Family Tree

The study of family history—genealogy—appeals to many of us. For some people, genealogy is an all-consuming pastime that takes them to distant lands and cities, introduces them to new relatives, and provides answers to questions about their personalities. For others, just finding out basic family history and background is enough.

You can start building your own family tree. First, see if anyone in your family has already collected materials such as family photos, letters, birth records, etc. Assemble information in chronological order, making notes about missing information. Add current facts about your own family: names, birth dates, cities or towns lived in, and so forth.

Then contact your oldest living relatives and see if they can fill in any gaps. You might use a family Bible or photo album to help jog their memories. Record their contributions, including references to stories you may want to follow up on later.

With this as a beginning, check other sources for further information. (Several possible sources are listed in the box on page 10.) It helps to know where your ancestors lived when they arrived in this country. Places of residence can provide the key to a good search of archival information—census records; birth, marriage, and death certificates; as well as property records. In most cases, United States records will indicate the country of origin as well, and

further searching can help you find records in those countries. Be aware, however, that many European records were lost or destroyed in World War II, and many country's boundaries have changed over time.

People choose different ways to collect and present their genealogical information. Some families keep a notebook with letters, records, and a family tree outline for each family member. Others use a preprinted form and fill in blanks on the family tree, then frame the result. Some family Bibles have a place to record basic family information. Several computer software packages allow you to design your own family tree.

Time Capsule

Have you ever wondered what life was like for people in your family one hundred years ago? How about what life will be like for your family one hundred years from now? Why not make a family time capsule so future generations won't have to wonder about your lives?

Time capsules have been around for thousands of years, and they have provided us with exciting information about different times and cultures. The actual term *time capsule* is more recent, however. It was coined by someone at Westinghouse Electric and Manufacturing Company as a name for a sealed container buried during the 1939 World's Fair. This time capsule contained artifacts and information about life in the first half of the twentieth century, and was designed to be opened in 5,000 years!

Your family time capsule probably won't last 5,000 years, but it will be fun to look at in the future—whether you make the "opening date" one, five, or fifty years from now. In fact, you may want to create a "New Year's Time Capsule" each January 1 and open it the following January 1.

To begin, determine what container to use as your time capsule. If you plan to open it within one or two years, a sturdy cardboard box will work. If you plan to keep the capsule intact for many years, consider a footlocker or sturdy plastic storage container.

Ask every family member to decide on things they will add to the capsule—a toy or book, a school composition or test, etc. (See suggestions in the shaded box.) Choose things that will reveal interesting things about you and your family. Make or purchase identification tags to write the date, name of the contributor, and the item, then attach the tags to the objects.

In addition to the individual items, consider adding a sheet of paper with everyone's age, height, and weight, as well as recent photos.

Once everything is ready, pack the time capsule carefully and seal it with strapping tape. Make a label for the outside of the container that indicates when it is to be opened, and have all contributors sign their names. Store the capsule in a safe, dry place until the big day arrives!

Ideas for the time capsule . . .

+ handwriting samples, autographs, or letters
+ photos and snapshots of all kinds
+ vacation postcards
+ art or craft items created by family members
+ favorite food labels
+ a TV listing for the week
+ a daily newspaper
+ pictures of sports teams, favorite actors, and singers
+ a list of hopes and dreams for the world in the year the box will be opened
+ an audiotape or videotape of a family event

Picture a Family Quilt

Everyone enjoys the beauty and warmth quilts provide; and quilts are genuine works of art—often the result of many people's efforts. Here is an idea for a unique family photo quilt that will provide beauty and warmth, the enjoyment of shared efforts and time together, *plus* a wonderful reminder of family roots.

Use the fabric requirements and assembly directions for the Hands-Down Family Quilt on page 20. Instead of painting handprints, however, you will transfer photo images onto the quilt blocks.

Plan your quilt design and choose related photos to copy onto the design. You might want a theme quilt: family trips, first days of school, Christmas celebrations. Or you might include individual portraits in a family-tree format.

Photocopy the pictures and use these copies for the quilting process. Many copy machines will let you reduce or enlarge the photos to a consistent size.

Purchase an image transfer or photo transfer solution at a craft or fabric store. Follow manufacturer's instructions to transfer the photos to a plain, white, cotton fabric, then proceed with arranging and sewing your quilt. Don't forget to add the name(s) of family members pictured in each square—either embroidered, stitched, or printed with permanent marker.

To complete the quilt, create a special tag or square with the embroidered, stitched, or printed names of the people who helped create the quilt, plus the date on which it was made. When the quilt is finished, follow any special instructions for laundering, and display the quilt where everyone enjoy it.

Made by Louise and Helen Gray 2/17/99

A Living "Family Tree"

Choose a special day and plant a family tree! Perhaps on Arbor Day, a birthday, or an anniversary, gather with your family to plant a tree in your yard. Take a picture of your family standing beside the freshly planted tree holding a sign with the date and everyone's name. Then take a picture of your family beside the tree each season of the year. Keep a "Family-Tree Album" that records the changes and growth in the tree and in your family!

Where in the World?

Do you know where your family came from? As our world becomes more similar in culture and tradition, it is important to learn and pass along things that make our family roots unique. Once you know where your ancestors came from (and it may be more than one country), find books, maps, and magazine articles about the countries. Designate a "family roots center" where you post a map, pictures, and books about the countries. Mark significant cities on the map, and trace routes your ancestors may have traveled during moves.

Choose a holiday such as Christmas or Easter and find out how it is celebrated in your countries of origin. Try to incorporate these celebrations in your own observances. If the country has a special national celebration day, mark it on your calendar and plan a family celebration of that day.

Family Fun Facts

Some of the most popular boxed games of the recent past include *Monopoly, Pictionary,* and *Trivial Pursuit.* Each of these games takes group effort, communication skills, and knowledge about the people you play with.

Why not create your own family variation of these games to help you get to know one another better? One easy way to begin is with homemade cards. Check an education supply store or catalog for blank playing cards, or use large index cards. Print a colorful design and the name of your game on the back of the cards, and questions or information on the front of the cards.

Memorable Moments

who was your first date?

NAME CARD

MOM

Family Fun Facts requires two stacks of cards: one stack contains the names of players—one name printed per card. The other stack contains questions, set up in categories.

Question categories should be fairly broad, but actual questions will be more specific. Some starter categories and sample questions you might want to include are provided on page 15.

Add any other categories and questions that you want. You should have no more than five cards per category—one question per card—and no more than twenty cards in all (to begin with).

To play the game for the first time, shuffle all question cards and place them, questions down, in the center of the table. Let each player draw a card, read the question aloud, provide the answer for him- or herself, and return the card to the bottom of the stack. Go through the stack of cards as many times as there are players—so everybody gets a chance to answer each card. *And be sure everyone listens carefully to the answers!*

Then shuffle all the question cards and again place them, questions down, in one pile. Shuffle name cards and place these, names down, in a second pile. The game now begins.

In turn, each player draws two cards—a question card and a name card. The player must answer the question *about the person whose name was drawn.* This requires good listening and memory skills. Anytime a player draws his or her own name, of course, it's a bonus. After each turn, cards are returned to the bottom of the stacks.

Set a time limit in which to answer the questions, and score a point for each correct answer. The player with the most points after the first round is the winner. Then shuffle the stacks and play a second round.

It is fun to keep adding question cards through the years, and the game makes a wonderful way to recall and share the past at family gatherings or reunions.

Sample Questions and Categories

✦ **Memorable Moments**

What month were you born? What was one thing that happened in the world the year you were born? What was the best vacation you ever had? Who was your first date?

✦ **Facts and Figures**

What was your first address and phone number? What are the complete birth dates of your father and your mother? What is the age at which your father got married?

✦ **All Creatures Great and Small**

How many pets did you have when you were growing up? What was the name of your mother's pet? What is one creature that scares you?

✦ **Holiday Happenings**

What is your favorite holiday? What would you most like to get for your birthday? What is the best gift you ever received?

Faith of Our Families

For hundreds of years, the family Bible has been a place where births, marriages, and deaths were recorded; where certificates of dedication, baptisms, or confirmation in the church were kept; and even where special flowers or locks of hair were kept as mementos.

Today, many homes have more than one Bible, and these often come in many versions—one for every family member! The large family Bible is no longer common as the keeper of records and memories. Perhaps it is time to reinstate this tradition—with a few contemporary twists!

If you have a large family Bible, encourage everyone to add their favorite Bible verses, prayers, and experiences of faith to pages designated for such records, or print these out on a computer and keep the pages in a special faith-journal notebook. (Then take time to read and talk about those entries with one another.)

One family I know values their baptismal certificates so much that they have framed and hung the documents in the entryway to their home. Many faith documents from the past—baptismal, confirmation, wedding certificates—are works of art that would look beautiful if framed and hung near photos of the people they represent. Perhaps a wall of family photos and certificates would make an interesting display in your home.

Be sure to add family faith stories to the stories you tell around the dinner table or at family gatherings. Talk about the time when Grandmother brought neighbors to faith by her words and deeds of witness, or the time an uncle silenced an angry mob by talking about Jesus' love, or tell about the time when your family had its prayers answered in a most remarkable way.

What's in a Name?

Your name says something very special about you. Your given, or "Christian," name was chosen by your parents, perhaps in honor of a special person or to remember something that happened the year you were born. Family names (surnames) are often handed down from one generation to another, sometimes directly and sometimes as middle or second names. Surnames often reflect a country or group of origin and express something about the original bearer of the name.

What are the given names in your family? Do you know the stories behind them? Were you named after one of your relatives? Someone in the Bible? Does anyone else in your family have the same given name?

To do research on your name, check the public library for or purchase a book of names. Such books will list traditional names with their variations, as well as origins and definitions. Some books even list pertinent or related verses for names derived from the Bible.

Your family name—usually your last name—often has a story to tell as well. Sometimes you can trace your family name back to distant relatives, or actually find a coat of arms or symbols from heraldry that identified your family. If you don't have a coat of arms or heraldic symbol (and most of us don't), it would be fun to create your own family logo, flag, or symbol to use on business cards, letterhead or stationery, bookplates, or as a family-album cover.

- ✦ Some families used a decorated letter as their logo.
- ✦ Ranches marked livestock with a brand that sometimes incorporated the family name into the ranch name.
- ✦ If you are Scottish or Irish, you might have a family plaid that is still worn to identify your family.

Notes

Genealogy Resources

Books:

Websites, Keywords:

People:

Our Family Places of Origin

Cities:

Countries:

Our Family Names (Surnames) and Meanings

MAKING MEMORIES

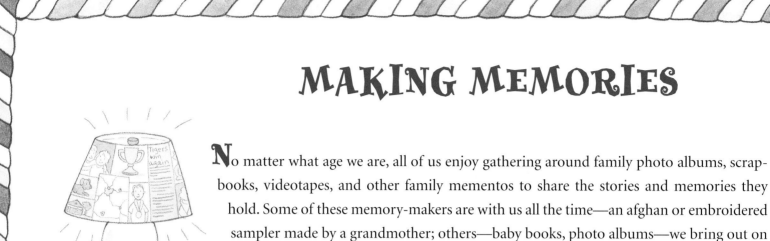

No matter what age we are, all of us enjoy gathering around family photo albums, scrapbooks, videotapes, and other family mementos to share the stories and memories they hold. Some of these memory-makers are with us all the time—an afghan or embroidered sampler made by a grandmother; others—baby books, photo albums—we bring out on special occasions such as birthdays or anniversaries. All these memory-makers add richness to our lives as they connect us with people and events from our pasts.

One of my treasured mementos is a bouquet of white ribbon roses. My mom saved the ribbon used in church when my husband and I were married and made it into a dozen white roses for our twelfth anniversary. I keep the roses in a vase that belonged to my grandmother. Mom and Grandma have given me many treasures, but these are my favorites!

Although it's fun to reflect on objects that recall special family times, it can be even more fun to create the mementos that trigger memories. Here are some idea-starters. Be creative! Look around! There are many things to turn into memories.

Hands-Down Family Quilt

A fun memento that everyone can contribute to is a handprint quilt. This could be made for your own family or as a special reminder of home for a family member away at college. It makes a great gift for newlyweds—with handprints of the wedding party or the families who are being joined. It's a perfect holiday gift for grandparents!

Supplies:
2 yards of cream or white fabric
1-¼ yards patterned fabric
2 yards of 60" wide Polarfleece
Fabric paints
Sewing needles
Thread or yarn
Pins (straight or safety)

Read through all the instructions before beginning this quilt. This pattern makes one quilt that has four blocks across and four blocks down. There are patterned strips between each block. For best results, use a sewing machine and a ½" seam allowance to piece the blocks and strips.

1. Cut the Fabric

Cut the cream or white fabric into sixteen 11" × 11" blocks. Cut twenty 11" × 3" strips from the patterned fabric. To make the long horizontal strips between the rows, cut the remainder of the patterned fabric into 3" strips from edge to edge. Sew these strips together end to end. Cut this long strip into five 3" × 53" strips.

2. Create the Handprint Blocks

A quick and easy way to make handprints is to paint each hand with fabric paint. These paints clean up easily and can be permanently set on the quilt blocks.

Using a soft brush, paint the underside of the hand, then spread the fingers apart and press down on the quilt block. Keep the hand away from the edges of the square by at least ½". Gently press down on each finger and across the back of the hand to make a good, clear print on the fabric. Carefully lift the hand straight up so the paint doesn't smear. Follow manufacturer's directions to set the paint so it will be permanent.

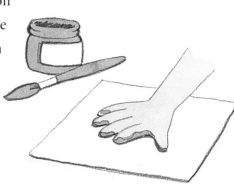

3. Assemble the Quilt Top

Lay out the top of the quilt. Sew the blocks and the 11" × 3" strips into rows first.

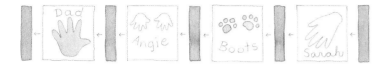

Then sew the 3" × 53" strips to the rows.

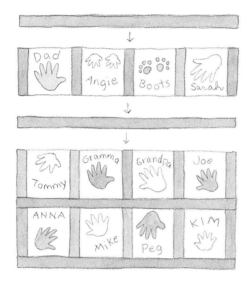

Lay the top of the quilt, right side down, on the Polarfleece. Pin together. Trim the Polarfleece to match the size of the quilt top. Sew the Polarfleece and quilt top, right sides together, on three sides. Turn right sides out. Hand or machine sew the fourth side closed.

4. Finish the Quilt

Now you're ready for a family quilting bee! Thread several needles with thread. Stitch around the blocks or the handprints, or create fun designs. If you would rather tie your quilt, thread a needle with lightweight yarn. At the corners of the blocks, bring the needle down through the quilt top and Polarfleece and up again. Tie a knot on the top side of the quilt.

Hints and Idea Starters

+ Don't forget your pet's prints.
+ If you don't want painted handprints, use fabrics to create the hands. Appliqué them to the blocks.
+ To embellish the hands or the wrists, add lace ruffles as a cuff or a ribbon for a ring.
+ Let everyone choose a favorite color for their handprint.
+ Add the name, date, and the age of each person beneath the handprint. Use a fine-tipped permanent marker or embroider the information on the block.

Mark Your Place

Historic buildings often have a marker by their entryways that tells visitors when the places were built, who lived in them, or some interesting information. Families might want to add such a marker to their homes—a plaque that lets visitors know who lives inside.

SMITH HOUSE
Joe, Katherine, Liza and Jennie moved here in 1993.
"As for me and my house, we will serve the Lord."
Joshua 24:24

Make a door plaque that includes your family's name, a special date you want to commemorate (when you moved in, when children were born, when you joined a church), and perhaps a favorite Bible verse or faith symbol.

Check a craft or hardware store for a wood, metal, or plastic base—maybe in an oval or shield shape. If it needs painting, choose a light color and add details with a contrasting shade. In addition to the information on the front, add the date and everyone's signature to the back of the plaque.

Memory Lamp

A bedside table lamp is a good place to keep memories. Having a memory lampshade by your bed each night allows you to remember pleasant things and have sweet dreams.

To make a memory lampshade, cover a plain paper shade with photos, maps, or other reminders of people and good times. Make photocopies of photos or heirlooms, then cut the copies apart and arrange them as you would like them on the lampshade. Brush a mixture of one part white glue and two parts water over the lampshade's surface, then position the photocopies around it. Cover the shade with the glue mixture after the pieces have dried in place and re-coat if necessary.

You might also buy a lamp with a clear glass base and fill this with treasured mementos: sand and seashells, special rocks or pinecones, or tiny baby toys.

Family Letter Book

Some families keep treasured letters. These might be letters from Mom and Dad's courtship, correspondence with relatives overseas, letters from a soldier in the war, or even letters home from a college student.

It is a good idea to preserve family letters. To do so, create a family letter book. First, make photocopies of the letters, as the originals will fade or become damaged with time. Type or word process a copy of each letter if the handwriting is difficult to read. Once you've made copies of these treasures, assemble them under clear acetate on pages in a scrapbook or three-ring binder. Bring the family letter book out to read together on special days and family events.

Fit to a "T"

If family members have been involved with sports teams, theater presentations, charity runs or walks, or even if you've just taken vacations together, you probably have drawers full of favorite T-shirts! Turn those T-shirts into something you can use and enjoy every day.

Sew the armholes and bottoms of the shirts closed, then stuff with polyester filling to make plump pillows. Finally, stitch the neck openings shut and toss the completed pillows onto a sofa, bed, or chair.

If you have many shirts, you might cut out the front panels to make the centers of quilt blocks. Piece and finish as you would any quilt. A quilt of sport-themed panels would make a great graduation gift for high school athletes leaving home to attend college!

Box It Up!

It isn't easy to know which childhood treasures to save. Who knows which mementos will have special meaning in future years?

One way to make sure you save mementos from everyone's childhood is to purchase an inexpensive box (preferably with a lid) for each child. Add one or two items every six months or each year on the child's birthday. A memory box not only acts as a memory-jogger to parents, it also keeps items safe in one place.

Items for the box might include school photos, a rock from a special hike, a club pin, a favorite sports card, or a poem or story the child wrote. Be sure to add a tag to each item with a date and other relevant information, or else tape a sheet inside the box lid, identifying and describing items.

Hand-Me-Down Mementos

Sometimes we inherit a box of items from a grandmother, favorite uncle, or distant cousin, and we don't quite know what to do with what's inside. That's where the fun begins!

Use some of these ideas to create mementos with hand-me-down things.

Grandpa's Ties

If you inherit a collection of old ties no longer suitable for use, turn them into a colorful vest, a couch throw, or even a stuffed animal! Ties can also be unfolded and sewn together, with the smaller point to the center, to make a sunburst pillow or tablecloth.

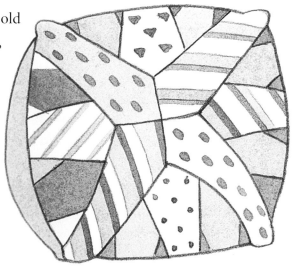

Baby Shoes

If you still have a child's first pair of soft baby shoes (or inherit your own baby shoes from your parents), cross-stitch the baby's name and date of birth on a piece of cloth, stuff the shoes, and fit the cross-stitched piece into the shoe openings. What a great heirloom Christmas tree ornament!

A Memory Wreath

Start with a wreath base, perhaps made of twigs or vines. Choose accompanying ribbon or trim to wrap around the wreath, then use a glue gun to attach mementos to the wreath in a pleasing manner. For example, if you have a box of buttons and sewing notions from Grandma's sewing basket, use seam binding or a tape measure as the ribbon, and attach spools of thread, buttons, a pin cushion, thimble, and so forth around the wreath.

Souvenir Specials

Have you ever come home from a vacation with more in your suitcase than when you left? This is known as the souvenir syndrome—and you're not alone! Here are a few ideas for what to do with those souvenirs.

Postcards-to-Go

Although it is more fun to take photos of vacation spots that include family and friends, sometimes the best pictures of the mountain or the trail are found on commercial postcards. Before a trip, give everyone a ring clip (used to hold papers together) from the stationery store, and take a hole punch along. As you purchase favorite scenic postcards, punch a hole in each and attach the cards to the rings.

Manila-Tag Treasures

Before you leave on your trip, purchase a package of manila tags, a glue stick, and a felt-tip pen for each person. Family members can record information about the trip or glue items on the tags—a neat way to keep mementos in one small space.

Family Scrapbooks

Have you been bitten by the scrapbook bug? If you haven't, I bet you know someone who has. Scrapbooking may be one of the fastest-growing hobbies today, and there are stores, parties, and classes offering to teach you how to make the most of family memories and that stack of photos.

The appeal of a scrapbook over a photo album is that you have more room to add extra touches that tell more of the story. Some people add stickers or cutouts to scrapbook pages. Words and stories in the style of journal or diary entries can also be added. And mementos such as ticket stubs, invitations, napkins, and thank-you notes can add details to the stories the pictures tell.

Here are a few ideas for themes and organization tips to help get you started!

Possible Scrapbook Themes

Family dinners	Birthdays
A book tailored to	Holidays
each family member	Vacations
School days	Crafts
Baby's first year	Hobbies
Weddings	Gardening

Tricks and Tips for Family Scrapbooks

+ Acid-free paper is best for preserving valuable photos and keepsakes.
+ Black-and-white photos keep better than color photos, so slip a roll of black-and-white film into your camera once in a while.
+ Organize papers, stickers, and other mementos by categories in plastic storage bags. Keep them in a portable hanging file box until you add them to the book.
+ Jazz up photos by cutting them in unique shapes (trace around a cookie cutter) or cutting parts of the photo out.
+ Sort photos by categories in a photo box. Don't be afraid to keep "bad" pictures—these can be great additions because you can cut these into interesting shapes.
+ As you work on a page, keep supplies for it in clear page protectors (available at office supply stores).
+ Identify people and places with a permanent pen. You may forget names.
+ Don't try to fit all photos for a time period in one album. Make several albums that feature different themes, or make one for each person.
+ Store albums in a cool, dry place away from direct light.

Remember-Me Wall Hanging

My three daughters wore matching holiday dresses in their younger years, thanks to the nimble sewing fingers of my mom. Along with the great holiday pictures we have from that time, I have saved small pieces of the fabric and plan to make each of them a small, quilted "Remember Me" wall hanging.

To make your own wall hangings, choose fabrics significant to you and cut a heart shape from each. Appliqué each heart to make the center of small quilt blocks. Border the blocks with white or unbleached muslin, and embroider the words "Remember Me" at the bottom of each block.

Notes

Our Special Mementos

Memory Boxes for _____, _____, _____, _____

Items for each box:

Scrapbook Themes

Materials needed:

PHOTO FOLLIES

When people are asked what things they would try to save first in the event of a fire or flood, most mention family photos and mementos. Photographs are irreplaceable treasures because they hold some of our dearest memories.

Photos also have an amazing way of accumulating until they overflow our shelves and storage spaces. Despite all our good intentions about sorting, labeling, and organizing them into albums and collections, there never seems to be time to get to that project. And so they pile up.

Here are some enjoyable and easy ways to make the most of your family photos, along with tips for planning and preparing for special photos you will want to take. Of course, many books and magazines offer even more ideas for the photography buff. You might want to check them out for additional ideas.

Family Photo Collections

A family photo book of a special event such as a wedding, birthday, baptism, anniversary, or holiday is a great way to store memories of that event.

There are as many types of photo albums as there are families, and you will want to browse in stationery and gift stores to find one that's right for you. Consider purchasing an album with a plain cover that you can personalize with paint, fabric, colored paper, and a family photo.

Here are tips to help you as you create or add to your photo collection:

+ Print names, places, and dates in album margins with a permanent felt-tip pen.

+ Store negatives or an extra set of prints of irreplaceable photos in a safety deposit box. Or send extra prints to a parent's or sibling's home for safekeeping. In case of fire, your irreplaceable photos won't be lost.

+ If there's a favorite place in your yard, gather the family there to take a photo each year. You'll have a record of changes and growth in your family and in your yard.

+ Choose interesting backgrounds. A great Christmas-card photo showed children bundled in colorful winter jackets and sitting in front of a stack of firewood. The background of weathered firewood made a beautiful contrast with their young faces and colorful jackets.

+ Organize photos in file boxes as soon as you have them developed. You can assign categories by the dates, events, or people in the photos. Or make up your own system!

Sharing the Days

Everyone needs a calendar, and everyone is guaranteed to love a calendar especially designed just for them. Many photo shops or copy centers will be happy to help you create a calendar gift for family and friends that features your children, your family, or your pets. (You may even purchase computer software that lets you create your own calendar at home.) Take photos that highlight something unique for each month of the year, or choose ones that show ways your family changes and grows.

To finish off your calendar with another unique touch, note special days you and the recipient celebrate: birthdays, anniversaries, holiday parties, planned vacations, and so forth. Then give your calendars as one-of-a-kind Christmas or New Year's gifts.

School Days

School pictures make great memories. You can use either photos you take yourself or the official school photographs. First-day-of-school snapshots taken by Mom or Dad as children climb aboard the school bus or as they pose with lunch boxes on the front porch are fun to collect. Both the professional school photos and the do-it-yourself shots make good gifts to share with relatives and to frame and hang in the stairway or hall.

One unusual way to display school portraits is in a long, narrow frame placed horizontally above a built-in cabinet—or vertically, down the side of a cabinet or cupboard. Make or buy a frame that fits the space and holds the number of photos you have. Then arrange school portraits in chronological order for each child. It is easy to see at a glance how everyone has grown. This makes a great year-by-year gift for grandparents. The first year, give them a frame and the first picture; each following year, add the new school photo.

Watch Me Grow

Some families use door frames as a kind of permanent growth chart, marking each person's name, height, and date at regular intervals. A variation on this tradition is to add a small photo, such as a school portrait, to each entry on the door frame. If you want to keep the growth chart should you move, tack a thin strip of wood or yardstick onto the door frame before recording information. It will be easy to remove the wood strip or yardstick if you move.

"Rogues Gallery" Photo Wall

A variety of family photos—old, recent, formal, or casual—displayed in a collection of interesting frames, makes a great "rogues gallery" for everyone

to admire and enjoy. First, determine if you want photographs of only your immediate family or photos that trace one or both sides of your family history. Then choose a pleasing number of photos, and match these up with frames that will enhance the overall look.

In an arrangement of similar photos, it's usually best to use similar-colored frames. If you can't find the color frames you want, why not paint them yourself? Your local hardware store has products that can make marbled, tortoise-shell, or even antique-looking frames. Give your frames a three-dimensional, sculpted look by gluing on buttons and other objects. Then paint them with the color you choose.

Or, for an entirely different look, decorate frames to fit the photos. For example, glue crayons around the frames of school children or place antique buttons on the frames of ancestors' photos. The frame of a pet dog's picture could be finished by gluing on small dog bone biscuits. Once you get started, the possibilities are endless!

Take a Picture

Some artwork and school projects take many hours to complete yet are difficult to store for the future. If your children's projects are beautiful but difficult to keep, why not keep pictures of them? Take photos of your child proudly holding the sculpture, papier-mâché project, or mobile, and display these in a special scrapbook of their work.

Suspended in Time

Sometimes, a photo tells only part of the story. Why not add telling details to photos and capture the whole story inside a frame? For example, group a child's baseball team photo with a ticket to a game, a scorecard, a newspaper clipping, and an individual photo of the child at bat. Or frame a dance recital picture with a program plus a piece of ribbon and tulle from the ballerina's dance costume. The photo of a gardener in his or her garden hat would look great alongside an empty seed packet and a pressed flower or two.

Capture these "stories" between two sheets of glass or Plexiglass and metal clips. Check a frame shop or art store for this type of framing system. Make sure the glass is clean and dry on both sides, then position the picture and items in a pleasing manner on one piece of glass and carefully lay the second glass over the top. Clip the panes together to complete the frame.

Notes

Themes for Family Photo Collections

Pictures to Take This Year

Who	_When_	_Where_	_Props_

WHAT'S COOKING?

Planning and preparing favorite family foods with fresh ingredients can be rewarding, not only for the cook but also for those who enjoy every bite. And special recipes, shared cooking experiences, and favorite foods are wonderful family hand-me-downs! You're sure to have memories of favorite childhood foods—and most likely you've also got a collection of favorite recipes handed down from your parents.

This section will offer some fun and unique suggestions about family cooking, tips on organizing and using recipes, menu idea-starters, a few recipes from my own family collection, and (I hope) the inspiration to find new and interesting ways to make mealtime enjoyable for the whole family.

A Family Cookbook

If you have a lot of cookbooks and a lot of favorite recipes from a variety of sources, you might want to assemble your own family cookbook collection. It can pay off in saved time and better meals. And it will someday make a priceless family hand-me-down!

For my family cookbook, I use a 3-ring notebook covered with clear plastic. The plastic covering allows me to create and insert my own book cover—a photo or a sheet I've made on my computer—and to add a title to the plastic-covered spine. Office supply stores also sell index dividers and clear plastic sheet protectors for the interior pages.

I divide my cookbook into categories that work for my family: Crock-Pot meals, salads, cookies, and so on. I began my first notebook by sorting the magazine clippings of "recipes to try," tossing any that no longer sounded good, and placing the "keepers" in a pile to try out and file. Those that I had tried and liked were placed into sheet protectors and slipped in my book.

I also included a page in each section where I noted tested and favorite recipes from other cookbooks, along with the name of the cookbook and the pages where they were found. This saved a lot of time when I couldn't remember where to find a certain recipe. Although I had a recipe card file, I found it was helpful to add cards I used most often to this notebook, too—slipping them between the sheet protectors in the appropriate sections.

- Other cookbook categories might be "FAVORITE MEAL MENUS—BRUNCH, LUNCH, DINNER."

- Some people write comments next to recipes they try, especially if they have varied the ingredients; or they note the date and guests who enjoyed the recipe.

- Sometimes my family rates a new recipe with a star system—5 stars is best and a definite "keeper." If a recipe gets less than 2 stars, we toss it.

Menu Magic

Planning meals and menus can be a challenge, especially for busy families. Some of the tips here may help your menu and meal planning. Add your own thoughts and don't be afraid to change plans after a few months. Remember that variety is the spice of life!

Planning Tips

+ Muffin tin meals. When small children won't eat, fill cups of a muffin tin with small portions of food. It makes eating more fun, and nutritious foods like raw vegetables can look appealing when served in individual compartments.

+ Post a calendar with the "menu of the week." It might ease moans and groans that accompany certain meals if everyone sees the bigger picture for the week.

+ Involve the whole family in mealtime planning, shopping, preparation, and cleanup. Have everyone choose a favorite meal. Schedule each person's meal on a day when they will have time to help prepare it.

+ Remind everyone to eat five servings of fruits and vegetables each day—their five fingers can be a reminder!

+ Share a meal! Sometimes families with similar schedules trade one night of cooking a week. On a designated night, one family prepares double food portions and takes half to a neighbor; the neighbor returns the favor another night. (Why does food almost always taste better if someone else makes it?)

+ Plan ahead. Occasionally make an extra meal to freeze, then heat and serve on a busy night.

+ Make a rainbow meal. Brighten up the plates with a variety of colorful foods. The most colorful foods tend to be fresh fruits, vegetables, and whole grains—foods that have the most nutritional value.

+ Set a pleasant table. The best dishes and silverware, along with flowers and candles, should not be just for guests! An attractive table makes even a simple meal a feast.

+ Learn several family table blessings to share each mealtime. Let everyone take turns choosing a favorite.

Family Favorites Collection

Use a three-ring notebook with section dividers to create an "everybody's favorite" collection. Let family members create their own sections in which they copy favorite recipes, tell what they like about each, and when they most enjoy eating it (holidays, breakfasts, snacks, etc.). Ask each person to sign his or her name, add the date and, if they feel artistic, an illustration of the food. A variation on this idea is to collect family members' favorite meals—complete menus—including recipes for each food served, a time or event when the meal works best, date, and signatures. These cookbooks make wonderful keepsakes, so you might want to duplicate pages and make an "everybody's favorite" collection for each member of the family.

A Break in the Day

In some cultures, time for tea, coffee, or snacks is built into daily work routines. Supplementing smaller meals with healthy snacks is a better way to keep up your energy than eating two or three large meals a day. Create your own family snack time or "happy hour" routine to break up the day and ensure that you keep your energy and nutrition levels high.

Happy Hour

If your family's evenings are often filled with activities, you might want to introduce a "happy hour" tradition after everyone has returned home from school and work—before dinner and the busy evening begins. This could be a time for cheese and crackers, a simple salad, or an appetizer that leads into the dinner meal. Top off your snack with juice or a juice spritzer (juice with sparkling water) and enjoy this chance to share the day's news and catch up with one another's lives.

Teatime

For teatime, keep a tray set with a teapot, cups, saucers, spoons, and a plate for cookies, biscuits, cheese, or fruit. Add sugar, creamer, or lemon slices if you like. To make a good pot of tea, first warm the pot by pouring in hot water, swirling it around, and pouring it out. Then measure the tea (loose, in a tea ball, or in tea bags) and pour hot water over it. Put the lid on and add a tea cozy to keep the pot warm while the tea brews. When the tea is the strength you like, remove the leaves or bags and pour it into teacups!

Many herbal teas are quite tasty, and even children will enjoy them. Be sure to try some of them, and experiment with teas that use herbs from your garden as well!

Cookie-of-the-Month

If you have a favorite cookie recipe, why not start a cookie-of-the-month tradition? Collect cookie cutters in shapes that have significance for your family or for special days or seasons of the year. Then make a batch of those favorite cookies in a new shape each month. Or wrap the cookies individually in plastic wrap, freeze them, and pull them out for lunch boxes at different times of the month.

Candy Creations

Your children won't remember the days when, if they wanted candy, families had to make it themselves—homemade taffy, fudge, and nut brittles. (In fact, you probably won't remember those days either!) But, if you talk to grandparents and great-grandparents, they may have fond memories of candy-making evenings with their families.

When I was young, my mom taught me how to make peanut brittle. This became a favorite pastime for us—one that also resulted in perfect gifts for birthdays and Christmas.

Check with your family. Is there an old candy recipe that you could make and share? If not, check cookbooks for a tasty recipe, or try this recipe for nut brittle, using your choice of nuts.

Nut Brittle

Ingredients:

2 cups sugar

1 cup light corn syrup

½ cup water

1 cup butter (*not* margarine or a butter blend)

3 cups (12 oz.) raw nuts—cashews, peanuts, macadamia nuts, or almonds

1 teaspoon baking soda

Grease two baking pans and set aside. Combine sugar, corn syrup, and water in a 3-quart saucepan and heat over medium heat, stirring until sugar dissolves. Bring the mixture to a boil and add the butter, stirring until it melts. Clip a candy thermometer to the inside of the pan, then reduce heat to medium-low. Continue stirring as the mixture boils at a moderate rate, until the thermometer reads about 280° (soft-crack stage).

Add nuts, stirring constantly, until the thermometer reads 300° (hard-crack stage). Remove pan from the heat and slip the thermometer off. Quickly stir in the baking soda, then pour the mixture into the buttered baking pans. As brittle begins to cool, stretch it out to edges of the pan by lifting and pulling from the sides with wooden spoons. As soon as it cools enough to touch, loosen brittle from the pans and break it into bite-size pieces. Store in a tightly covered container or plastic storage bag.

For Dandy Candy

- Cook all candy recipes to the specified temperature.

- Try to make candy on a dry day; humidity may keep candy from hardening.

- Use a wooden spoon to stir your candy.

- Always use butter unless the recipe says otherwise.

- Grocery stores sell tiny paper candy cups—nice containers for sharing your treats.

- Make tasty candied fruits by melting white or dark chocolate cubes and dipping half a fruit like apricots or fresh strawberries into the chocolate. Allow to cool on waxed paper.

- Fill a pastry bag with warm, melted chocolate and write a name or message (such as "I love you") on waxed paper. Peel chocolate off when it dries. Now you have a personalized candy note!

- Wash and dry herb leaves (such as mint) from your garden. Brush the leaves with melted chocolate and let them harden on waxed paper. Carefully peel chocolate from the leaves when it cools. Store chocolate leaves in the freezer to decorate cakes or other special desserts.

Do-It-Yourself Foods

We no longer need to work as hard as our ancestors did to preserve food. In fact, many of us may never have seen a pressure cooker or canning kettle. But nothing can beat the flavor of strawberry jam you made yourself from berries you picked or of apples you have dried and stored in the snack jar. A lot of the enjoyment from such treats comes from the hard work and good memories that went into creating them—a rewarding task *and* a tradition to hand down!

If you want to try canning, drying, freezing, or pickling foods, many books at the library or your local bookstore can serve as your guides. You may need to buy or borrow special equipment for each method you try. Be sure to follow instructions regarding cooking times and temperatures so the food is preserved correctly and safely.

Many of the following recipes and ideas are ones my own family enjoys. Because of our busy schedules, we have limited time, so these are fairly quick and easy methods. Some of these are ways to preserve a bit of summer for our winter months; others are for preserving foods and drinks that can be enjoyed any time of the year.

Frozen Fruits and Vegetables

Plan a time for fruit and vegetable picking, then freeze some of your harvest for the winter months. One easy way to do this is to wash the fruits or vegetables, let them dry, then spread them on a flat baking sheet and pop the sheet into the freezer. After the produce has frozen, it will be easy to scoop off and store in the freezer in a plastic storage bag. I use this method with grated zucchini. I measure the frozen zucchini into mounds that are the right size for recipes I plan to use. I bag and store each mound individually.

Herb Butter

Pick and wash your favorite herbs to make herb butter. Chop these as fine as you like, then mix them with softened butter. You can pat the butter into a mold or small dish, or roll it into logs. Wrap the herb butter in clear plastic wrap, then again with foil or freezer paper and label each packet. Remove as much as you need to use with baked potatoes, warm sourdough bread, or anything you can think of!

Frozen Herb Cubes

Freeze portions of your favorite fresh herbs, such as basil, thyme, mint, or lemon balm, in water inside ice cube trays. It is easy to add a frozen herb cube to a pot of soup or sauce, or a mint cube to a cup of tea.

Make Your Own Butter

Despite what some people may think, butter does not start out as yellow sticks at the grocery store. Even if you don't have access to a butter churn, your family members can make fresh butter at the table and then eat it with their meals.

Wash and dry the small plastic canisters that film comes in, then pour heavy whipping cream into each container, filling it half way. Have everyone shake his or her container and, after about ten minutes, a lump of butter should form in the liquid. Pour the liquid out and use the butter on warm bread. (This butter has no color or salt added, and it will taste sweeter than butter you are probably used to.)

Lavender Sugar

Blend sugar and fresh or dry lavender buds in a grinder or blender. Use in tea, cookies, or other baked goods.

Scented Geraniums

One of my favorite plants to grow and enjoy is the scented geranium. These flowers are different from the bright red geraniums we usually think of, and they are valued for their leaves rather than their flowers!

Scented geranium leaves are most often used in pot-pourris, but it is also fun to bake with them! And their flavors include chocolate, mint, and lemon.

To make a scented geranium cake, lay several clean, dry geranium leaves on the bottom of a greased cake pan. Pour the batter in carefully, so the leaves remain flat. After baking and cooling the cake, invert it onto a cooling rack. Sprinkle powdered sugar over the top, leaving the outline of the leaves visible. Then carefully remove the leaves. The scent will remain in the cake, and the leaf design is lovely!

Sun Tea

It's easy to make sun tea, even if the sun isn't shining! Fill a large clear jar or pitcher with water and 4-6 tea bags or, if you'd like herbal tea, use a handful of fresh herbs. Try a mixture of herbs, such as several mints and lemon balm, lemon verbena, or pineapple sage. Set the jar in the sun or in the refrigerator for half a day or so. When the color of the tea indicates it's done, remove the leaves or tea bags. Enjoy with a slice of lemon or lime, honey, or sugar to taste.

Sun tea is usually not as strong as brewed tea, and it's a relaxing way to make a large quantity.

Fruity Syrups

It is easy to make great fruit syrups for pancakes and ice cream toppings. First cook the fruit in a small amount of water until juices begin to flow. Press with a wooden spoon to help squeeze out juices, then pour the fruit and juice into a food processor or blender and blend. To every 1-½ cups of fruit juice, add 1-½ cups of sugar. Return the syrup mixture to the stove and bring it almost to a boil, stirring until all the sugar dissolves. Store in the refrigerator or pour into bottles and seal.

Almost Maple Syrup

Bring 1 cup of water and 2 cups of sugar to a boil, stirring constantly. After sugar has completely dissolved, stir in ½ teaspoon of maple flavoring. Cool and store in the refrigerator.

Orange Syrup

Boil 1 cup of orange juice and 2 cups of sugar for 1 minute, then stir in 2 tablespoons of lemon juice. Store in the refrigerator.

Garlic and Onion Braids

The easiest way to store garlic and onions is to gather a bunch, tie them together at the top, then hang them to dry. But it's more fun—and the result is much more appealing—to make a braid to hang and dry, cutting off garlic heads or onions as needed for cooking. Start with three stems that are similar in length and braid these together just as you would braid a child's hair. Continue the braid, weaving in new pieces before you run out. Attach a ribbon or twine bow for hanging, and tuck in dried flowers for a decoration at the top.

Snow Cream

Snow ice cream is a great winter treat, although it may take a trip to the mountains to find snow that's fresh and clean.

Method #1: Empty a can of evaporated milk into a chilled bowl (set the bowl in the snow first to chill it). Add two to four tablespoons of sugar, a dash of salt, and a generous helping of vanilla, instant coffee grains, or sweet cocoa. Quickly stir in fresh snow, tasting and adding more flavoring as needed, until you get the right consistency. Enjoy!

And now two methods for when you can't find clean snow!

Method #2: Pour 1 cup of whole milk into a small plastic storage bag. Add 1 teaspoon of vanilla and 1 tablespoon of sugar. Then seal the bag. Put about one dozen ice cubes into a large plastic storage bag and sprinkle about 2 tablespoons of salt on the ice. Nestle the smaller bag into the ice in the larger bag and seal it. Shake the bag for at least ten minutes or until you begin to notice ice crystals form in the milk mixture. When the milk is about the consistency of soft-serve ice cream, open the bags and enjoy!

Method #3: Pour milk or cream into a small can with a resealable plastic lid. Add a dash of sugar and vanilla, then close the can and seal the lid with sturdy packing tape. Place the can inside a larger can with a lid, packing ice around it. Sprinkle salt on the ice, then put the lid on and seal with packing tape as well. (Now you need family teamwork!) Roll the tin-can package back and forth or around in a circle. Eventually, you will have ice cream!

Notes

Recipes to Get from Grandpa and Grandma

Family Favorites to Note in Cookbook

Resource Books for Cooking, Freezing,
Canning, and Pickling

THE GREAT OUTDOORS

Running through the sprinkler on a hot summer day, raking huge piles of autumn leaves and then jumping in them, decorating an outside tree with Christmas lights, planting backyard flower and vegetable gardens—we all have favorite memories set outside in God's beautiful world. And whether you live in a city apartment, a suburban housing development, or a farm in the country, you can make wonderful family memories in the great outdoors.

The rhythm of seasons can sometimes become so familiar that we don't stop to think how blessed we are or stop to enjoy them. Perhaps some of these ideas will remind you of childhood family traditions, or maybe they will inspire you to make new traditions with your family. Most of all, I hope they lead you and your family to more fully appreciate and enjoy the world of wonders outside your window!

Walk This Way

Walking is perhaps the easiest and most beneficial exercise. Best of all, we already know how to do it! It isn't always easy, though, to get everyone off the couch and moving in the right direction. If suggestions to walk the dog or get a little after-dinner exercise don't get any takers, try some of these fun ways to start a family walking habit.

Rainy-Day Splash

How about a walk in the rain and a splash in the puddles? My family and I live in a part of the country notorious for gray, rainy days. The rain isn't always a downpour; in winter it's usually just a gentle mist that doesn't even require an umbrella (at least not for native residents).

When our children were small, and we felt cooped up inside for too long, we would take rainy-day walks, complete with rain slickers, boots, and umbrellas. We set out with the express purpose of walking in the rain and splashing in every puddle we found. My daughters thought this was great fun. In fact, about ten years later, they still think so. Just the other day, after a stretch of gray, wet weather, I found Morgan out on the deck, tap-dancing and blowing bubbles in the rain

Rainbow Walk

Before beginning your walk, choose a favorite color. As you walk, see how many things of that color you can spot. During your walk you might want to expand your list to include all seven colors of the rainbow!

Flip a Coin

Designate a "coin tosser" for all or part of your walk, and give him or her a penny.

As you reach each corner or turning point, toss the coin. Let someone else call heads or tails and, if the call is correct, choose which direction to go. (If the call is wrong, the "coin tosser" decides.) Or designate a direction for each toss—heads, right; tails, left. This is a fun way to vary your walking path and discover new sights.

Sandy Castles

A trip to the beach or even the sandbox isn't complete without building a sandcastle or two. Here is a way to bring the sand castle fun into your own home.

For a small castle, you will need about 1 cup of sand, ½ cup of cornstarch, 1 teaspoon of cream of tartar, and ¾ cup of hot water. (You can easily increase the amounts as you enlarge the size of your sandcastle.)

Mix dry ingredients in a saucepan, then add the hot water. Heat on medium flame, stirring constantly as the mixture thickens. Remove from heat when it gets too thick to be stirred and let it cool to the touch. Then build your sandcastle. Allow the castle to dry for several days. Store leftover sandy clay in an airtight plastic bag or container for another project.

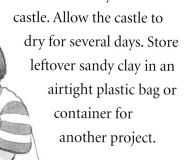

An Heirloom Garden

Wouldn't it be nice to preserve and pass along favorites from the garden—flowers and plants that have special meaning for you and other family members? It's possible! You can create your own "heirloom garden" by saving seeds and starter-shoots from favorite plants, and share and trade with friends and family.

To collect "heirloom seeds," why not make your own packets? Use small manila or waxed paper envelopes, print the name of the seeds on the front, notes about where the plants grew, when you usually planted them, tips for proper care, and so forth. You could even take a photo of the plant or have someone draw it for the front of your seed packet.

When the weather is dry and warm at the end of summer, watch for mature seed heads on favorite plants, then cut the heads off. Open the seed heads over a sheet of paper and let the seeds dry in a cool, well-ventilated place for two or three weeks. After they dry, fill your seed packets and wait for next spring to plant them again!

Some plants aren't easy to start with seeds, and you'll need to make cuttings. If a plant roots easily, make a clean cut of a stem and place this in a jar of water. Watch it carefully until it roots, then plant it in soil.

Other plant cuttings need to be dipped into a hormone root powder. Check with a greenhouse for the types of plants that require this. After this step, you can plant the stem in a small pot of soil, cover it with a plastic bag or glass jar, and keep the soil slightly moist until roots form.

Check a greenhouse, gardening store, or gardening books about the best way to preserve your favorite flowers and plants.

For the Birds

I've heard that bird-watching is one of the most popular outdoor activities today. There are certainly plenty of opportunities to find out about and try this fun hobby.

No matter where you live, you will find birds that can provide hours of entertainment for you and your family.

One way to attract birds for watching is with a bird feeder or birdhouse. Here are unique bird-feeding stations and shelters your family can create.

A Bird-Feeder Wreath

It is easy to make a wreath feeder that your backyard birds will enjoy. Purchase or make a twig wreath and insert seeds, sunflowers, and other bird favorites into the twigs. Or spread peanut butter or suet on the wreath and sprinkle with birdseed.

If you feel ambitious, form bread dough into a wreath and insert seeds in the top. After it bakes, hang the wreath outside where the birds will enjoy it. You can "reseed" the wreath after birds have nibbled by spreading peanut butter or suet over the top and pressing in seeds.

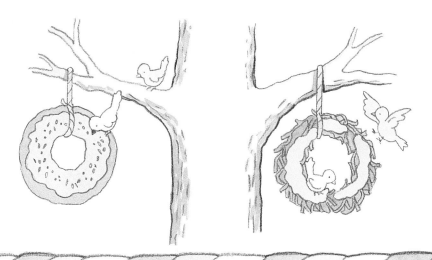

Check your local library, the National Audubon Society, or a nature or garden store for classes, tours, bird walks, and other nature events offered in your area.

Drip, Drop

A homemade birdbath is a nice addition to your backyard bird sanctuary. Use a plastic plant draining saucer as your "bathtub," and place several large rocks in the bottom for birds to perch on. Add water and place the saucer on a level, elevated surface, such as a tree stump or post. Prick several tiny holes into the bottom of a plastic liter soda bottle, fill it with water, and suspend it above the birdbath. The "drip-drop" of the water will attract birds to the bath, and will help keep the saucer filled—if you keep the bottle filled!

Grow a Gourd House

Gourds are the odd-looking fruits sometimes grown for their unusual shapes. If you can grow gourds, you have the beginnings of great houses for birds!

Follow seed packet instructions for growing. Harvest gourds before the first frost, cutting them off the stem. Wash them carefully, then drill a small hole through their necks. Insert wire to suspend the gourds and allow them to dry for about four weeks. You will know the gourd is entirely dry if you can hear seeds rattling inside when you shake it.

To make your gourd house, use an electric drill to put a 2" hole in the side for a door. Scoop out seeds or fiber. Then drill several ¼" holes around the bottom for drainage and ventilation. To help preserve the gourd, spray it with two coats of polyurethane or varnish. Use the drying wire to hang the finished house. Sit back and wait for the arrival of new homeowners.

Squash in a Jar

Surprise your family with this amazing trick! Once the yellow blossoms appear on squash vines, watch for the tiny young fruits. The best ones to use are at the bottom of the plant, where leaves will make shade and keep the squash from growing too big. Slip the tiny squash into a jar. (You can ensure shade by placing a folded sheet of newspaper over the jar.) When the squash almost fills the jar, cut it from the vine. Screw the lid back on the jar and impress your family with "bottled squash"!

Personalized Pumpkins

Grow pumpkins with your name on them! After the young fruits have appeared on your vine, use a small, sharp knife to carve your initials or name into the side of a pumpkin. As the pumpkin grows, your initials will grow, making an unusual personalized addition to your fall harvest.

Rock Collecting

Rock collecting is something most children do at one time or another. Why not make it a family adventure? Some of my favorite memories of my grandfather are times we searched for agates together on the beach and then waited while his rock tumbler washed and polished the stones shiny and beautiful.

Family rock hunt hikes are a great way to learn new things about God's wonderful earth as you collect beautiful souvenirs. To help you get started, check out a library book about rocks and minerals. Find a sturdy container for your rock collection: check a craft or hardware store for a plastic box with small compartments, like a small tackle box. Include a magnifying glass for inspecting the rocks you find and small stickers to label them. Every time you take a walk, you can find rocks to inspect, classify, and label.

There are basically three classifications of rocks: *metamorphic* (formed by pressure, heat, and water); *igneous* (the result of volcanic action); and *sedimentary* (formed by deposits of sediment).

Worlds of Ice

Don't let the cold and snow of winter keep you inside! Build an ice castle, carve an ice sculpture, or make ice luminarias to light up your garden path.

The basics for building with ice are simple and inexpensive. Of course, freezing temperatures are a prerequisite. Once you've got that, collect a variety of household containers, such as buckets, plastic food tubs, milk jugs or cartons, gelatin molds, muffin tins, Bundt cake pans, funnels, plastic liter soda bottles, egg cartons, bowls, and yogurt containers.

Fill the containers with water and set them outside to freeze. Add food coloring to some containers if you want a stained-glass effect. When you have enough containers frozen, briefly dip them into a pan of warm water and slide the ice out. To join the ice shapes, spray flat surfaces lightly with water and press the shapes together, holding them a few seconds until they freeze together. Then let your imagination go wild and create beautiful worlds of ice.

Ideas for Your "Worlds of Ice"

+ a castle with turrets
+ an ice dragon
+ a shimmering luminaria, made by stacking ice blocks in a circular shape (igloo fashion), and placing a candle inside

Pressed Flowers

One of my grandmothers had an old, old dictionary—the biggest I'd ever seen! My brother and I always had fun searching through that dictionary—not for words, however, but for the pressed flowers and leaves Grandmother had hidden between the pages.

The easiest way to preserve flowers is to pick them at their peak and carefully press them between pages of a heavy book or beneath several books. You can also make or buy a flower press, which is usually two same-sized pieces of wood with a screw and wing nut in each corner. Flowers are placed between sheets of paper and positioned between the top and bottom boards; then the wing nuts are tightened to press the flowers flat. After about three weeks, the flowers have dried and are ready to use.

Pressed and dried flowers can be used in a number of ways, some of which are illustrated here.

Here are tips for drying and preserving flowers:

+ Pick flowers early in the day, if possible.

+ Press the flowers right after you pick them so they don't start to wilt.

+ Flowers that usually press well include pansies, bachelor's buttons, violets, buttercups, Queen Anne's lace, and individual hydrangea blooms. Ferns and leaves also press well and add a different look to the completed projects.

+ Arrange leaves and petals carefully before you press them.

Backyard Olympics

If you live in a neighborhood where everyone knows one another, here's a great way to make those relationships even stronger. If your neighbors don't know one another, here's a way to introduce everyone!

Plan a "Backyard Olympics" with each backyard hosting an event, such as tug-of-war over a water hose, a game of croquet, a badminton competition, or even a plain old jump rope extravaganza. Or, if you have a large backyard, designate a section of your yard for each event. Share a barbecue or potluck dinner when the games are finished.

And to make the day even more fun, have a presentation of certificates or medals—made from metal juice-can lids. This might even turn into an annual event!

Stargazing

There is something special about watching the stars outside late at night. This family hobby can be as much fun as bird watching; and anytime little children have an excuse to stay up late, they are thrilled!

Find a book with guides to the night skies or constellations in your part of the country, and decide on the best time of the year for stargazing. In many parts of the country, August is a great time: nights are nice and warm, and often, about mid-month, there are incredible meteor showers to observe.

Wait for a clear night. Then spread a blanket or quilt on the lawn or set up garden chairs and gather the entire family. Use a pair of binoculars or a telescope, if you have them, to better your stargazing. A tub of popcorn or cups of cocoa will add to the appeal. You might even begin a stargazing journal to keep track of the constellations and night-sky phenomena you see!

Notes

Good Reference Books about . . .

Birds   Gardening

Rock Collecting   The Night Sky

Names and Phone Numbers of Neighbors
(Backyard Olympics and Barbecue)

Name	Phone Number	Activity/Food

SPECIAL WAYS FOR SPECIAL DAYS

It's easy to remember and celebrate the "big days"—Christmas, New Year's Eve, Easter. There are reminders all around us, from the media and merchants and our own specially-marked calendars. But any day we have a chance to celebrate with family and friends is a great day.

I believe God created every day as a special day. We need to make sure we enjoy and appreciate each one. Stop and think about ways you can help make each day special. Do you ever leave a message to congratulate a friend? Have you sent a note to thank a teacher for a job well done? Or baked a special treat for your family "just because"? If you ever do anything to make an ordinary day a little brighter, you are already finding special ways to make special days. On the following pages are more ideas to add to your collection!

Dinosaur Days

Have you or other family members ever gotten really immersed in a fascinating topic? Then you know what it's like to eat, breathe, and sleep the topic. Why not turn such interests into theme days?

If your children are fascinated by dinosaurs, for example, make the most of it. Rent videos about dinosaurs, find library books about dinosaurs, make dinosaur-shaped pancakes for breakfast and dinosaur cookies for an after-school snack. Find out what plants certain dinosaurs ate, and mark a map to show where dinosaurs may have lived. Use clay or plaster of paris to make "dinosaur-fossil" paperweights. Make dinosaurs the theme for a day, a week, or even a month at your house.

Dinosaurs are just one topic that intrigue children. What are others? What are topics that intrigue you? Ask everyone in your family to list fascinating topics and then plan ways to build theme days into a year of learning about new and different things!

Theme-day starters

Plants of the Bible, shipwrecks and pirate ships, safaris and circus animals, great art masters, ancient architecture, calligraphy, foreign cultures and countries, favorite authors and their works . . .

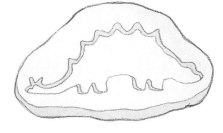

Bike Parade

Plan a neighborhood bike parade that is fun to ride in and fun to watch. Advertise that on a specified day you will host a bike parade, concluding with a block barbecue or ice cream social. Check with local government offices about blocking off your street for this event. Sometimes, cities and police departments sponsor activity days to focus on neighborhood involvement in crime prevention. This might be something you could plan in conjunction with the parade and barbecue.

Decorate bikes, wagons, scooters, and strollers by wrapping crepe-paper streamers around handles and leaving the ends free to blow in the breeze. Weave colored streamers in and out of the spokes on bike wheels to make a colorful pinwheel.

When my brother and I were young, we loved to attach playing cards between our tire spokes with clothespins. What a great clicking noise it made as we rolled along!

To keep the parade moving smoothly, use chalk or taped paper arrows to mark the path. Take lots of pictures and have music playing as the parade rides by. Line up all the featured bikes, wagons, and strollers at the end of the parade and take a group picture. Then enjoy a potluck dinner, barbecue, or ice cream social.

Smile!

Even if it hasn't been a particularly good day, funny-face pizzas will make everyone smile. Give everyone half an English muffin to use for his or her face. Spread a tomato- or pizza-sauce base on the muffin, then add toppings to create a face. Pepperoni rounds make great eyes; green pepper strips can be eyebrows or a nose. Add a tomato-slice smile and sprinkle cheese "freckles" around the features.

After everyone has made one or more faces, toast the muffins in a 350° oven for 5-7 minutes or until the cheese melts. Have fun eating the faces—and SMILE!

From Birthday to Birthday

If you have a video camcorder, start a birthday video for each person, adding to the videotape every year. This is a fun way to see the growth and changes in a person, and it's fun to watch as the years pass. Be sure to include the person's age and date on the videotapes each year!

Birthday Memory Book

Make or purchase a special book for each family member, one with blank pages on which to store birthday memories. Decorate each cover with each family member's name and birth date, then designate several pages for each year's birthday. Include a list of the birthday celebrant's favorite things for the year, his or her age and physical characteristics, the birthday meal and cake, and names of guests if there was a party. Take pictures of the celebration and add these, plus school or church photos, to the memory book.

Your Golden Birthday

We know a family who has added a unique celebration to their birthday traditions. They call it the "golden birthday," and it takes place when your age matches the date of your birthday. For example, if you were born on the twelfth of the month, your twelfth birthday is your golden birthday.

A yellow cake would be appropriate for that birthday—topped with golden icing and candles. Gold or yellow balloons and crepe paper would make perfect decorations. Birthday wrapping paper could be gold foil. And how about planting a patch of yellow daffodils or buying a yellow rosebush as a gift?

Mug-of-the-Day

Some families use a "you-are-special-today" plate to honor someone who has a special day. Why not adapt this idea and have a "mug-of-the-day" for someone who deserves an extra pat on the back, or (maybe even better) who has had a string of bad luck?

Choose a cheerful mug, perhaps one that says something like, "I think you're great!" or one that has a smiling face on it. Prepare a favorite hot drink, such as flavored tea or hot cocoa, add a garnish—a fruit slice or marshmallows. You can print a brief Bible verse or cheery message on a paper flag and attach it to a beverage stirrer. What a great way to start a special day!

Silly Supper Night

Sometimes our mealtimes are so predictable. Create a little excitement and plan a "silly supper night"! Serve foods that are normally never served for supper, such as breakfast cereal, ice cream cones, and popcorn; or make it a meal of favorite snacks and hors d'oeuvres: chips and vegetables with dip, little wrapped sausages, crackers with cheese. Set your table in a silly place too—maybe have a picnic in the car or a candlelight dinner in the basement.

A silly supper night can be so much fun, you might want to make it a monthly event!

Special-Day Tablecloth

Many families have beautiful table linens they use only on holidays and special occasions, and everyone gets terribly uncomfortable trying not to spill on them. How about creating a special-day tablecloth that can make ordinary meals and ordinary days extraordinary?

Choose a light-colored tablecloth that fits your kitchen or dining room table (whichever table you use for everyday meals). Every month or so, give everyone a pencil and let them draw pictures, handprints, or doodles—or write messages—on the tablecloth, then trace over their additions with a fabric pen or paints. Following the manufacturer's instructions for these materials, dry or heat set to make the designs permanent. By adding pictures or doodles to the tablecloth, you will be building extraordinary family memories.

First Day Fun

In the Old Testament book of Ecclesiastes we read that "For everything there is a season" (3:1). Here are ways you and your family can welcome the seasons and make the first day of each season special.

Fall

Eat a fresh-picked lettuce-leaf salad. Run through a pile of leaves. Polish the boots and shoes in your closet. Make a table centerpiece with pumpkins, gourds, leaves, and squashes. Bake pumpkin muffins. Drink a mug of warm spiced cider.

Winter

Make snow cones with shaved or crushed ice and your favorite fruit juice. Clean out the freezer. Bake cookies to eat with a cup of hot cocoa—don't forget the whipped cream and sprinkles on top! Buy a new pair of gloves or mittens for everyone in the family; have everyone put them on and take a picture with everyone waving!

Spring

Bring a branch into the house and "force" it into bloom by pounding the end with a hammer, then putting it into a bucket of warm water by a sunny window. Clean your closet. Wash your windows. Hang a wind sock outside your window. Go fly a kite!

Summer

Go wading at the beach or in a park fountain. Plan a picnic in the park. Take a family picture beside—or in—a swimming pool. Buy new inexpensive plastic sandals for everyone and decorate them with paints, fake flowers, or glued-on plastic "jewels." Buy everyone funny sunglasses and take your pictures as you lie on the sand. Gather your neighbors together and play a pick-up game of baseball.

Notes

"Special Days" to Remember Each Month

January   February   March   April

May   June   July   August

September   October   November   December

LET'S TALK

The statistics are alarming, and they don't seem to be improving: families no longer spend much time talking together. Even the tradition of the family meal together seems to have gone by the wayside. Pagers, cell phones, and answering machines have replaced face-to-face communication. And with the schedules we keep, often the only times we have for conversation are in the car on the way to an event, to sports practice, or to a music lesson. Even those of us with the best intentions must really work at finding ways to talk about important things with our families.

On these pages you'll discover some fun ways to keep talk flowing in your home. Try them out and talk up a storm!

Mealtime Modeling

Our family is probably no different from yours when it comes to mealtimes. We have tried to keep the dinner hour sacred. But despite our best efforts, dinnertime is often rushed, and our conversations are far from enlightening.

Like all parents, I wanted to know how my kids' day at school had gone—what they had done and learned. But my dinner-hour question—"What did you do today?"—was usually answered with "Nothing." After a few days of this, I used Mom-psychology and turned the tables on my kids.

"Guess what *I* did today!" I would announce. I'd then proceed to describe everything I could think of that I had done or read or learned that day. This worked just as I had hoped. My children decided they didn't want to spend the entire time listening to me, so they began telling me the things they had done or read or learned. Soon, most mealtime conversations were flowing along nicely. (Of course, it was only a few weeks into this pattern before Lindsay, our oldest daughter, sat back with a smug look and announced, "I know what you're doing, Mom!" Oh, well. At least it worked.)

Remember: listen with your heart!

Celebrate-a-Blessing Book

Why is it easier to gripe and complain than it is to appreciate the blessings from God we encounter each day? Start a family book to celebrate your blessings, and you will have a treasure to read whenever you feel blue.

Your book could be a spiral notebook or a journal of handmade paper. Title your book "Our Celebration of Blessings" and ask everyone to think of at least two blessings a day to write or draw in the book. At first, everyone will probably be eager to contribute, but as time passes they may lose interest or forget. Be sure to leave the book in a spot where people will be reminded to add to it each day.

Take turns reading the blessings aloud in a family gathering at least once a week, and include some of those blessings in your family prayers.

Question-of-the-Week

Everyone goes to the refrigerator at least once a day. That's why the refrigerator door often becomes the message board or "command central" for so many families.

Take advantage of its visibility by posting a "question-of-the-week" on the refrigerator door. Encourage everyone to think about and answer it before the week is over. If you have a white board with magnetic backing, mount it on the refrigerator and leave a dry erase marker nearby for people to note—and initial—their answers. (A chalkboard or piece of chart paper would work, too.)

You might pose a variety of questions such as: What is your all-time favorite dinner? What birthday gift would you most like to receive? What is one nice thing someone did for you today? What is your favorite Bible story? or What is your biggest pet peeve? Let everyone take turns adding a question of the week.

Use this board to lead into dinnertime discussions of favorite things, values, friendships, faith, God—and a host of other topics. Let the question-of-the-week open discussions on subjects such as family vacations, an impending change in your family (a new job for Mom, a new baby, a possible move), current events, the environment, your church, or even political decisions.

Family-Thought Notebook

Everyone has favorite quotations, bumper-sticker slogans, or Bible verses. And even though we have our own understanding of these words of wisdom, it would be nice to share those understandings while getting other people's interpretations as well.

Buy or make a special notebook for this purpose. Begin by writing a favorite Bible verse or quotation on the first page. Then write what you think it means or how it speaks to you. For one week, leave the journal open in a place where other family members can read it and add their own thoughts. At the end of the week, meet together to talk about the quotation and the variety of meanings and responses to it. Ask everyone to take turns adding his or her favorite thought to the notebook.

A Day in Our Life

Does everyone in your family know what other family members do in a day? It can be a real eye-opener to keep a log of tasks and errands, games and pastimes, the small and large decisions, trips in the car, phone calls, questions you answer—even how much money you spend on things throughout the day. (And the log will probably surprise the person who's keeping it as well!)

Make a daily schedule sheet on which you divide up your waking hours into half-hour segments—either a sheet for each person or one large sheet to post on the refrigerator. Be sure there's room for everyone to accurately record the things they do in the day. Then plan an ice cream party to meet and share your days.

Dad	Mom	Jan
10:00 Computer Meeting	9:00 Volunteer at Book Fair	Book Report due today
	Lunch with Ronda 11:30	
3:30 Doctor's Appointment		5:30 Soccer Practice

I-Love-You Messages

How often do we tell members of our family that we love them? Try some of these quick and easy ways to cheer someone's day with these three words—*I love you!*

"I ♥ U" notes

- Lunchbox "I-love-you" notes are great written on napkins or shells of hard-boiled eggs.
- Pancake batter can be poured from squeeze bottles into the symbols "I ♥ U."
- Write "I love you" with small pebbles or stones along a flower bed or garden path.
- When the bathroom mirror steams up while someone is taking a shower, write "I love you" on the mirror.
- Make a cassette-tape message that includes a thought for the day and the message "I love you." Then secretly insert the tape in a car cassette player or set it off as a morning alarm clock.
- Place a favorite flower on the seat of a car before someone leaves for school or work.
- Leave an "I-love-you" message on an answering machine, pager, or as a screen saver on your computer.

Something New Calendar

Make monthly calendar grids do double duty by writing "Something I Learned Today" in bold letters across the top. Encourage everyone to add something they learned in the box for at least two days each week. Some items to add are: factual information, faith facts, or current events.

Keep the calendar as a record of the diversity and scope of family life and learning in a year. And flip through it as the year draws to a close or as part of a New Year's Eve celebration with family.

When I Was Your Age . . .

We've all probably heard a variation on the lecture, "When I was your age, I had to walk three miles to school every day." Unfortunately, we don't always know the countless other—and often fascinating—stories from the childhood experiences of our parents and grandparents.

Why not plan regular family get-togethers to share and enjoy "When I was your age . . ." stories? You might designate a recorder or "historian" who can capture the stories as they are told—either on audiotape, videotape, or by writing them down. Be sure to make copies for family members who would want to cherish these stories.

If it seems difficult to get people to tell their stories, try some of the following as jump-starts:

- Tell about the best thing that happened to you before you started school.
- Name and tell one thing about each grandparent, great-grandparent, aunt, and uncle who you remember.
- What is the best thing that happened to you when you were __ years old?
- What is the worst thing that happened to you when you were __ years old?
- What was your favorite Bible story when you were my age? Is it still your favorite?
- Tell what you know about the day you were born or adopted?
- What is a funny story you heard about your childhood?
- What is one holiday you'll never forget?
- What is your favorite family vacation?

Family Bedtime Story

Bedtime stories are a tradition in many households, and the best kinds are often those that are created in serial installments of one per night. These stories can be added to and enhanced by everyone in the family, and this collaborative effort is sure to increase family bonding.

Once a parent begins to tell stories, children often ask to hear them again and again. And if, like most parents, you're a little too tired at the end of the day to remember the story you told last week (or even last night), a story that you add to each night can rescue you *and* capture the children's interest. Their imaginations can take off if you invite them to help you create the next "chapter." Give it a try tonight!

How about a bedtime song that signals it is time to go to sleep?

One family I know uses the song "Silent Night" for their bedtime song all year. Maybe you and your family have another peaceful favorite that will work for you.

Bible Promises Book

Make a memory book of your family's favorite Bible promises. Choose a plain sketchbook from an art supply store or use a notebook filled with unlined paper. Let each family member print her or his favorite verse in bold lettering at the top or bottom of a separate page. Cut out magazine pictures or draw pictures to accompany your favorite verses. Make up games to memorize the verses as you add them to the book.

There is special comfort when a family has the same Bible verses to cling to in times of joy or sorrow.

I will lift up my eyes to the hills— where does my help come from?
Psalm 21

Week-in-Review

On Friday or Saturday evenings, play a game of "Week-in-Review" to answer the who, what, why, when, and where of each family member's week. Use a game board spinner or make your own, using a plastic coffee-can lid, a brass fastener, and a paper clip. Divide the plastic lid into five sections labeled: WHO?, WHAT?, WHY?, WHEN?, and WHERE?

To play "Week-in-Review" have everyone take a turn spinning the spinner. They must answer the question they land on by telling about something that happened to them during the past week. For example, if someone lands on "WHO?" they might tell about a new person who started in their class at school. As additional turns come to each family member, he or she can decide whether to continue talking about the event or person from the previous turn or introduce a new subject.

This is a fun, non-threatening way to find out how everyone's week went. And it can help families learn to be sensitive to the kinds of things that affect one another away from home.

Two Truths and a Trick

There is an old game called "Two Truths and a Lie." Although it is never a good idea to lie, the game can be fun if we change its name to "Two Truths and a Trick." The idea is to see how much people in a family know about each other and help them get to know more about one another.

To play, each person thinks of three things to share with the family. Two of the things will be true: things they have done or would like to do, things they have seen, people they have met, or anything about them that is true. One of the things they share will not be true (the "trick"). Each person takes a turn telling his or her three things, then everyone else takes turns guessing which are true and which is the trick.

The outcome can be hilarious, especially for people everyone thinks they know well!

Family Meetings

Regular family meetings can be a real asset to any family—times when everyone gets a chance to share thoughts and frustrations, gets advice and suggestions, works out strategies for better communication, discusses rules and restrictions, makes plans for special vacations, and takes part in decisions about other important family matters.

Family meetings can be as formal or as informal as you like. Some families find it helpful to trade off responsibilities of planning and running the meetings; while in others, there are definite rules about who takes on what role. It is a good idea to have a set day and time for the meetings—one that everyone in the family agrees to and honors. It's also often helpful to set some ground rules about how long one person can dominate a discussion or what topics are off-limits. Every family will need to set its own rules—and be prepared to see those rules evolve and change over the months and years, just as the family members and situations evolve and change.

It can be both helpful and fun to appoint a "recorder"—someone to take minutes for the meetings for future reading. These notes also can be helpful to settle any disputes that may arise! And be sure to plan an enjoyable activity or a food treat to share as part of the meeting. All work and no play makes meetings no fun!

Notes

Question-of-the-Week Starters

Places and Ways to Send "I-Love-You" Messages

Bedtime Stories and Songs

Family Meeting Ideas

Day and Time   Length   Regular Agenda Items

KEEP IN TOUCH

It isn't enough to keep in touch with only the family members who share our house; we've also got to find ways (and time!) to communicate with grandparents, uncles, aunts, nieces, nephews, cousins, distant relatives, and family friends. Today, as in the past, people love to get mail and receive phone calls with the latest family news. And, with all the technology today, it can be easier than ever before to keep in touch. That is, of course, *if* we take the time and make the effort to do so.

Many of us are good about sending off an annual Christmas card or letter, and some of us may even enjoy and look forward to that task. But there are other ways to keep in touch that may be even more fun— ways that could become family traditions handed down from generation to generation.

Family Newsletter

With the number of computers and assorted software programs available today, creating a newsletter to share with family and friends is not the chore it used to be. Check with your computer store for a program that can get you started, and then adapt and adjust the software format to fit your family. Once you've set up a layout for the paper, it's easy to flow in new articles for each issue.

First decide on some basics. Will your newsletter come in monthly or yearly editions? Will you include news of only your immediate family or of your family-at-large—including distant relatives and family friends? Who will be included on your mailing list? Can you feature photos and/or drawings in your newsletter? How about a regular calendar of upcoming family events: birthdays, weddings, anniversaries, graduations, moves, and get-togethers? What about including a favorite recipe of the month or for the season?

Once you've decided on the content, you can begin preparing the layout and writing about family events. (If you have a computer, this may be the easy part!) After printing your newsletter, send copies to everyone on your mailing list. And be sure to keep a notebook or file of newsletters for the "family archives"—a record of your family's comings and goings and doings throughout the years. Then check your newsletters for ideas about what to write in your family Christmas letter.

Christmas Cards and Letters

Some people enjoy nothing more than planning and sending out Christmas cards and letters. And whether you are one of those people—or someone who approaches the task less than enthusiastically—you can be sure that your cards and letters are appreciated.

Despite the jokes about Christmas letters, they are almost always read *and* appreciated. They are still one of the best ways to let people know what you and your family have been up to during the past year.

Here are ways to make your Christmas letter more enjoyable to create and read:

+ Have all family members write a paragraph about what the past year held for them or what they hope the coming year will hold. (Don't forget to include notes from your pets—ghostwritten, of course!)

+ Or designate a different family member to write the letter each Christmas. It's fun to get a varied perspective from year to year.

+ Write your letter on one side of a sheet of paper and make a montage of family photos for the backside. Copy both sides, and your letter is done.

+ Some families take a Christmas photo each year, sometimes with the family and pets gathered around the same chair or the same tree. This is a good way to record family change and growth. You might also want to create a photo that lets people know who you really are: take a photo of your ski vacation or with characters at Disneyland. Get everyone busy with yard work and take photos of them painting the fence or jumping in leaves.

+ Check out library books for ideas on making your own pop-up Christmas greetings or using rubber stamps to create unique cards.

+ What about printing your Christmas message on a simple homemade or purchased ornament of paper or fabric that can be mailed easily? Not only will your friends enjoy the special greetings, but they will also remember you each year they decorate their Christmas tree.

Round-Robin Letters

An old letter-writing technique that is great fun and doesn't take a lot of work is the round-robin letter. Each family who receives a round-robin letter reads it, adds their own letter, and sends the collection to the next name on the list. The last family on the list sends all letters (minus the first family's) back to family 1. The first family reads the collection, removes the second family's letter, and sends the rest on to family 2. Family 2 reads the collection, removes the third family's letter, and sends the rest to family 3. And so it continues until all families have read all letters. Every family gets caught up on all the news, and has to write only one letter.

Find a number of relatives or friends that want to participate with you, and then agree on a schedule that will keep the round-robin letter moving and the news fresh. For example, you start the letter on Monday and mail it by Thursday to make sure the next person has it in time to add a portion the following Monday. This is a great way to keep long-distance relatives and friends in touch with one another, and the shared nature of the letters helps to build a wonderful, close-knit community.

Family Reunions

A popular summer tradition, the family reunion is often the only time people of many generations and distant families come together to share their common history. Sometimes family reunions are built into weddings, baptisms, special anniversaries, or graduations; but reunions are often planned as unique events.

Here are suggestions that can help make the preparations easier and the reunion itself more enjoyable.

Date, Location, Budget

For your first family reunion, perhaps the hardest task will be choosing a date that works for everyone. After reunions become regular events, it becomes much easier: everyone plans ahead and blocks out the date. The scheduling also may depend on availability of the site where the reunion will be held. Will it be centered in a private home with nearby motels and a park, or will you stay at a resort or campground with cabins? Before checking on family schedules, find out dates when resorts, campgrounds, or motels are available.

Even if most events are held at a private home or local park, there will be expenses. A realistic budget is a must. Here are things to consider when planning your budget:

* Will you need to rent an indoor site—pavilion or tent—in case of rain?

* Do you have enough tables and chairs or will you have to rent these as well?

* Make meal-by-meal menus based on the number of people you expect; then check the paper for prices of food, drinks, plastic and paper ware (table covers, plates, knives, forks, cups), and estimate the cost per meal.

- Will there be rest room facilities or will you need to rent a portable toilet? What are the regulations for doing this?

- Will guests bring coolers and ice to keep food cold or will you need to purchase these? Will you need a barbecue grill?

- Don't forget to include the cost of invitations, stamps, and other materials that will be used in the cost-per-family breakdown. Some families like to create "memory books" or photo albums; others like to design a T-shirt to commemorate the event. Be sure to think about these things ahead of time and plan your budget accordingly.

- When you have a fairly complete cost estimate, divide it by the number of families who will be attending (don't forget to add lodging costs), and include this fee on the invitations you send out—along with a date for responding (with payment, if attending).

Travel and Lodging

If people will be traveling from another city or state, it is nice to send them a simple map or "travel guide," including interesting things to see and do in the area—in case they choose to extend their stay. You can usually obtain such maps and brochures free from a city chamber of commerce, business organizations, or map sites on the Internet. Include information about transportation to and from the airport, train, or bus stations.

Check to see if local motels will offer special rates for reserving a block of rooms during the days of the reunion. Find out about campground rates in case there are people who would like to camp.

Favorite Foods

One enjoyable part of a reunion can be the sharing of family recipes. It can take a large burden off the organizer if food preparations are shared by a number of family members (usually by those who live in the area). If someone is known for a favorite dish, ask them to bring it along. If not, give people the choice of a food category, such as salad or dessert, and let them bring whatever they'd like. It's a good idea to ask everyone to bring copies of their food recipes to hand out to family members, thus compiling a "family favorites" cookbook on the spot.

Family Fun

Although most fun comes from the visiting and the getting reacquainted, a few planned activities can help break the ice and keep things moving. How about a "This Is Your Life" skit that features each family acting out one fun memory they have?

Or have a family-fact quiz in which someone reads out facts connected to specific family members—significant dates (weddings, births, moves, etc.); places (hometowns, places of employment, schools, churches); names (teachers, pastors, best friends, bosses); and quotations (pet phrases, "famous last words," humorous expressions)—and everyone tries to guess who the person is.

A fill-in-the-blank family tree or genealogy notebook is a good way to help everyone see their connections to the larger group. Then find a place to make photocopies of the completed chart or book pages and hand these out to everyone before they return home.

Baby pictures brought from home can make a fun guessing game. Post the pictures on a wall and provide stick-on note sheets for everyone to make their best guesses. At the end of the reunion, identify all the pictures and declare the person with the most correct guesses the winner.

If there are musicians or actors in the group, ask them to present a mini-talent show. This can be a lot of fun, especially when people who haven't performed together for years team up for part of the show!

If possible, provide disposable cameras for everyone and encourage people to take pictures throughout the reunion. Then take the cameras to a one-hour photo studio, collect the pictures, and host a photo-album session. Let every family put together its own memory book of the reunion before they go home.

Prayer Notebook and Message Board

A prayer notebook or message board is one way to remind one another that God answers prayers. It's also a good way to help everyone keep in touch with one another. If you already have a central message board, you can use that. Otherwise, you could create a prayer book everyone can write in.

On the left-hand pages of the book, enter any prayer requests from, or your concerns about, people you know and love. Use blue ink to enter those prayer requests, and be sure to add the date of your prayer. When the prayers have been answered, record the answer and the date in red ink on the right-hand page across from the request.

It is always encouraging to look back and see the many times and ways that God has answered prayer in our lives.

Grandma/Grandpa Classes

A grandmother I know had several well-loved recipes that were always requested when there was a family get-together. One summer, she planned what she called "Grandma's Cooking Class" and invited her grandchildren to spend a week with her, learning to cook the family favorites.

Cooking isn't the only thing that can be taught at a class conducted by grandparents. How about making a quilt or knitting? Or how about making strawberry jam, planting a garden, building a birdhouse, or tying flies for fly-fishing?

This is a great way to share the knowledge and skills of family members, and it's an even better way to build understanding and communication between generations. A wonderful way to keep in touch!

Sweet and Simple Touches

Words aren't the only language we understand. We all know that sometimes actions speak louder than words. Here are great ways to keep in touch, with or without words, on a daily basis.

✦ Read the Bible and pray aloud with your family every day.

✦ When you send a special reminder note in a lunchbox or briefcase, fold it into a paper airplane or an origami shape. Add colorful hearts that say "I love you."

✦ Write a letter to your children every year on their birthday or to your spouse every year on your anniversary. Tuck it into their gift. Tell them how much they mean to you.

✦ Send your parents flowers on *your* birthday. After all, without them you wouldn't be here!

✦ Develop a special, secret sign or look that signals "I love you." Even as your children get older, this is something they will treasure; and, because it's just between the two of you, it will never embarrass them. When we leave my parents' house for the long drive home, our tradition is to honk "I love you" (three long honks) as we round the last curve of their driveway. They return the honks with a big wave, and we're on our way.

✦ Plant a tree or bush to commemorate a special day in a family member's life. Make a tag to note the date and occasion and attach it to the plant.

Notes

Our Family Newsletter

Articles and Writers   Regular Features   People to Mail or E-mail it to

Possible Sites and Themes for a Family Reunion

Ideas for "Grandma/Grandpa Classes"

JUST FOR FUN

Here is a hodgepodge of miscellaneous tips, tricks, games, and tales—ideas and activities that don't fit into any specific category, but are great family fun. And they're the kind of things that make perfect family hand-me-downs.

Enjoy trying these ideas. See if they trigger memories from your childhood: riddles, jokes, tongue twisters, campfire tales, winter fun, outdoor games for summer nights. At the end of this section is space to add your own "just-for-fun" ideas. Write them down so you won't forget them; then try them out together.

Tongue-Twister Tournament

Plan an evening of laughter as you experiment with tongue twisters! Here are some classics to get you started:

+ Rubber baby buggy bumpers
+ She sells seashells at the seashore.
+ Peter Piper picked a peck of pickled peppers.
+ How much wood would a woodchuck chuck if a woodchuck could chuck wood?
+ Eight gray geese grazed gaily in Greece.
+ Shoes and socks shocked Susan.

You can also make up some of your own. Decide how many times each tongue twister should be said (as fast as possible!) by each participant. The person with the fewest mistakes wins each round.

Build a Huck Finn Raft

Make a mini-version of Huck Finn's raft to float down a stream, in a lake, or even in a wading pool. Cut a bunch of sticks or twigs with at least two of them about two feet long. Lay the two longer sticks on a level surface, at least 6" apart, to form the base. Cut the remaining twigs to about 10" long and lay them across the base for the flooring. Starting at the center and, working toward both ends of the base twigs, glue the flooring to the base. For additional strength after the glue has dried, use fishing line to lash the flooring to the base sticks.

If you want a sail, wedge and glue a slender twig "mast" between two flooring pieces, and use string to attach a cloth sail.

Tin-Can Stilts

You will need two sturdy cans of the same size for each pair of stilts (coffee cans or quart juice cans work well). Open the cans at one end, flattening any jagged edges on the inside. Use a hammer and nail to make a hole several inches from the top on either side of each can. Tap down any jagged edges.

Cut two pieces of thin rope that measure about three times the distance from your knee to the floor. Thread the ends of each rope into the holes in each can—from the outside to the inside—and make a firm knot at each end of the ropes. When you pull the ropes taut, the knots will catch against the insides of the cans.

To use the stilts, step on top of the cans and pull the rope in either hand so that it stays taut. Then go for a stroll and enjoy your new height!

Paper Airplanes

Paper airplanes are fun to make and, if they're carefully crafted, can fly amazing distances. Some families even have competitions to see whose plane will fly farthest. You can find a number of books with directions for building unique, beautiful, and streamlined paper airplanes. Here are instructions for a "whirly plane" that is easy to make and fun to fly.

Cut out a 6-½" × 1-½" strip of paper. Form "wings" by cutting a 3" slit down the middle of the paper from one end toward the center. Fold "wings" back in opposite directions (see diagram) and attach a paper clip to the bottom of the uncut end. Then step on a chair, drop your whirly plane, and watch it spin!

Chalk It Up!

Sidewalk chalk drawings and hopscotch grids are childhood traditions. The great thing about chalk on sidewalks is that it washes off with a garden hose or the first rainfall.

Plan an "art gallery" competition among family and friends using sidewalk squares as picture frames. Or, instead of traditional hopscotch, try a gigantic version of ticktacktoe. Or play the following variation on hopscotch: "Snail's Pace."

To make a "Snail's Pace" playing area, draw a large spiral shape on the sidewalk. Label the center circle "Home," and divide the spiral path leading to "Home" into twelve spaces. To begin, the first person hops down the spiral from the outside toward "Home," landing on one foot in each of the twelve spaces, and on both feet in "Home." Then, hopping on both feet, the player turns around, shifts back to one foot, and hops back out—once again landing on each of the twelve spaces in the spiral. If the player manages this without stepping on a single line, he or she can write his or her initials in any space of the spiral. No successive players are permitted to land on that space. Play continues with players adding initials to a space of their choice if they don't step on a line. As the number of initialed spaces grows, the game becomes more and more challenging! When no one is able to reach "Home," the player with the most initialed spaces is the winner.

Shadows on the Wall

There's probably someone in your family who is an expert at making shadow pictures! If so, let that person teach you the art. If not, find a library book on how to make hand-shadow pictures. Then plan an evening of shadow plays. (All you will need is a light-colored wall and a flashlight.) Have one person shine the flashlight while the "director" creates wild creatures and funny faces. And, if you'd like, tell a story to go with your faces and creatures—turning the evening's entertainment into a shadow play!

House of Cards

Test your building skills as well as your steady hands and build a house of cards! Build a tower of cards. Or invite the family to help you construct an entire village! If you've got an old or incomplete deck of cards, you can simplify the task by cutting a short slit into the center on each side of the cards. Then it will be easy to interlock and connect the cards in all kinds of interesting structures!

Games That Never Grow Old

When you have a collection of favorite games, you've got the makings for wonderful family times—as well as treasures to hand down from one generation to another. The following golden oldies may remind you of your own childhood favorites. Be sure to add some other games you played as a child to the list!

Hide the Thimble

Choose a thimble or other small object to hide somewhere in a designated area such as the living room, dining room, basement, or garage. Show it to all the players before you begin. Then have everyone leave the room while you hide the thimble. Invite everyone back in to search. When they spot the thimble, they should sit down immediately without saying a word. It is easy to see who has and who has not spotted the thimble. The game continues until all players are seated.

A variation on the game is to have the hider provide clues as players search the room such as "You're getting warmer" (getting closer to the thimble); "You're getting cooler" (moving away from the thimble); "You're red-hot" (very near); or "You're ice-cold" (very far). The first person to find the thimble wins *and* gets to hide it in the next round.

Tag

Every family has a favorite version of this game, but here is one you may not know. It's called "Elbow Tag" and is best played with eight or more players. One person is designated as the "tagger"; one or two players (depending on how many are playing) are "runners"; all other players form pairs by linking arms and standing still. At a signal, the tagger chases the runner(s), who can get "safe" by linking arms with any of the standing pairs—making a threesome. *But* two is company, three is a crowd! And one of the original pair has to leave the new threesome to become a runner—and be pursued. Whenever a runner is tagged, he or she switches roles and becomes the tagger. Half the fun of this game is the confusion and panic that comes as roles change.

"Statues" is another fun version of tag. When "it" tags another player, the player must freeze—become a statue—and can't move until tagged by a player who is still free. The goal is to turn everyone into "stone"— except for the player who is "it."

Deal Me In

There are as many card games and variations as there are families, and some families have favorites that everyone loves. Why not invite the whole family—grandparents, uncles, aunts, and cousins—to a card-marathon evening? Find out everybody's favorite card game and incorporate these into the evening's marathon. Gather in groups of four around separate card tables, each offering a different card favorite. At designated times, break for cookies or popcorn, then reassemble at new tables with new partners for new games.

Here are some card games that are favorites with a lot of people: hearts, crazy eights, go fish, solitaire, spoons, war, blackjack, rummy, pit, euchre, and pinochle. Add your own favorites.

Kick the Can

This is a family and neighborhood game that's perfect for a summer evening. You'll need an empty can, a level and open surface for "base" (a driveway, a blocked-off street, or playground), and five or more players. The can is placed, open-side-down, in the center of a circle (marked off with chalk). The player who is "it" stands with one foot on top of the can and counts to fifty, while the other players scatter and hide in the area. After announcing "Ready or not, here I come!" the player who is "it" moves away from the can to hunt for the hiding players. As soon as he or she sees a hider, he runs back to the can, sets a foot on it, and calls out "Tin can down on [*name*]. I see you behind the oak tree [*or wherever*]." As players are caught, they must come in to base. The object is for the player who is "it" to spot and "tin-can-down-on" everybody. If that happens, the first person caught becomes "it" for a new game. *But* if one of the hiders sneaks in and kicks the can while the player who is "it" is away from base, all captured players are again free to run and hide while the player who is "it" fetches and returns the can. Then the game starts over.

Here are just a few more childhood favorites: Red Rover, Red Rover; Captain, May I?; Red Light, Green Light; and Duck, Duck, Goose. See if they trigger other games, and add your favorites to the list.

Notes

Our Favorite Childhood Games

Outside Summer Games

Winter/Snow Games

Types of Tag

Card Games

Board Games

Tongue Twisters